ISSUE NO. 266

U.S. Department of Justice
Office of Justice Programs
National Institute of Justice

I0448709

NIJ

National Institute of Justice

JOURNAL

NIJ Commemorates the 15th Anniversary of the Violence Against Women Act

- Perspectives on Civil Protective Orders in Domestic Violence Cases: The Rural and Urban Divide

- Men Who Murder Their Families: What the Research Tells Us

- Voices From the Field: Stalking

Also in this issue

Predictive Policing: The Future of Law Enforcement?

Making Sense of DNA Backlogs — Myths vs. Reality

Untested Evidence: Not Just a Crime Lab Issue

U.S. Department of Justice
Office of Justice Programs

810 Seventh St. N.W.
Washington, DC 20531

Eric H. Holder, Jr.
Attorney General

Laurie O. Robinson
Assistant Attorney General

Kristina Rose
Acting Director, National Institute of Justice

This and other publications and products
of the National Institute of Justice can be
found at:

National Institute of Justice
http://www.ojp.usdoj.gov/nij

Office of Justice Programs
Innovation • Partnerships • Safer Neighborhoods
http://www.ojp.usdoj.gov

NCJ 230409

NIJ

BUILDING
KNOWLEDGE TO
MEET THE CHALLENGE OF
CRIME AND JUSTICE

National Institute of Justice

Kristina Rose
Acting Director, National Institute of Justice

The *NIJ Journal* is published by the National Institute of
Justice to announce the Institute's policy-relevant research
results and initiatives. The Attorney General has determined
that publication of this periodical is necessary in transacting
the public business of the U.S. Department of Justice as
required by law.

Findings and conclusions of the research reported here are
those of the authors and do not necessarily reflect the official
position or policies of the U.S. Department of Justice.

All products, manufacturers and organizations cited in this
publication are presented for informational purposes only,
and their discussion does not constitute product approval
or endorsement by the U.S. Department of Justice.

Subscription information
online   https://puborder.ncjrs.gov/Listservs/nij/reg.asp
phone   301-519-5500
               800-851-3420
mail   NCJRS
               P.O. Box 6000
               Rockville, MD 20849-6000

World Wide Web address
http://www.ojp.usdoj.gov/nij/journals/welcome.htm

Contact NIJ
National Institute of Justice
810 Seventh St. N.W., Washington, DC 20531, USA
http://www.ojp.usdoj.gov/nij/contact/welcome.htm

NIJ Journal Editorial Board

Thomas E. Feucht
Executive Science Advisor

George Tillery
Acting Deputy Director for Science and Technology

Angela Moore
Acting Deputy Director for Research and Evaluation

Jolene Hernon   Nancy Ritter
Lee Mockensturm   Cheryl Crawford Watson
Marilyn Moses   Edwin Zedlewski

Editor
Philip Bulman

Contact the Editor
Philip.Bulman@usdoj.gov

Production
Palladian Partners Inc.

Jennifer M. Walsh, *Managing Editor*
Jill R. Grozalsky, *Production Coordinator*
Aaron Auyeung, *Designer*
Maureen Berg, *Designer*

Director's Message

Violence against women is an issue that is near and dear to my heart. Having spent almost six years at DOJ's Office on Violence Against Women, I gained an extraordinary appreciation for how the Violence Against Women Act (VAWA) has changed the lives of women and their families around the country.

The National Institute of Justice has played a significant role by funding hundreds of research studies on domestic violence, sexual assault, stalking and teen dating violence. In addition, NIJ is evaluating programs that aim to reduce violence against women. As we commemorate the 15th anniversary of VAWA, this issue of the *NIJ Journal* features several studies:

- Research about civil protective orders in urban and rural areas of Kentucky identifies the barriers women face in getting the orders as well as the overall effectiveness the order has on deterring violence.

- A summary of a seminar about men who murder their families and then commit suicide points out that a man's past behavior is the best predictor of his future behavior and that violence tends to escalate, especially when mixed with alcohol and guns.

- Findings from research about stalking is the topic of a guest column by Michelle Garcia, an expert on the topic from the National Center for Victims of Crime.

I would also like to draw your attention to two articles about backlogs of evidence in our nation's law enforcement agencies and crime laboratories. A newly released study documents the problem of evidence (including DNA evidence) being held in police custody. The separate issue of backlogs in crime laboratories is the subject of Mark Nelson's article. He shows that backlogs in crime labs are directly proportional to the incredible increase in demand for DNA analysis. He also includes information about several noted NIJ programs that help labs improve their capacity to analyze DNA.

Finally, I would like to point out an article on an evidence-based program for drug offenders. Rigorous evaluations of the Hawaii HOPE program show that the swift and certain approach to probation has significantly reduced recidivism rates, even among people regarded by probation officers as very high-risk probationers.

Kristina Rose
Acting Director, National Institute of Justice

NIJ

June 2010
NIJ JOURNAL / ISSUE NO. 266

Contents

Publications
IN BRIEF

Geography and Public Safety Bulletin
Volume 2, Issue 2: Neighborhoods

This issue discusses neighborhoods and the importance of geographic composition. It examines topics, definitions and technologies that demonstrate that neighborhoods matter. Articles bring the abstract idea of a neighborhood into a concrete set of issues for practice. The articles by Marc Buslik, Phil Canter and Mark Warren highlight how numerous delineations of neighborhood boundaries make it more difficult for the police to serve the public adequately. John Markovic discusses why neighborhoods matter when implementing community policing. Lastly, Jim Zepp highlights how residents of various neighborhoods participated in a government contest to create Web sites that helped citizens of Washington, D.C. better communicate information about their neighborhoods to others.

Articles include:

- Why Neighborhoods Matter: The Importance of Geographic Composition

- Not In My Neighborhood: An Essay on Policing Place

- Policing Neighborhoods in Baltimore County

- Neighborhoods Matter: A Situational Policing Perspective

- Applying Community Policing Tapestry Data to Public Safety

- The Socioeconomic Mapping and Resource Topography (SMART) System

▶ http://www.ojp.usdoj.gov/ nij/maps/gps-bulletin- v2i2.pdf

Events and Training Seminars

The National Institute of Justice co-sponsors events and training seminars about relevant and timely issues in criminal justice and technology research and practice.

Events

2010 Innovative Technologies for Corrections Conference
June 21-23
Fort Lauderdale, Fla.

The 11th Annual Innovative Technologies for Corrections Conference will spotlight existing and emerging correctional technologies.

Impression & Pattern Evidence Symposium
August 2-5
Clearwater Beach, Fla.

NIJ, the Bureau of Justice Assistance and the Federal Bureau of Investigation's Laboratory Division will co-sponsor this event.

For more information go to http://www.ojp.usdoj.gov/nij/ events/welcome.htm.

Training Seminars

Course	Date	Location
Advanced DNA Technologies	7/19-7/23	Huntington, W.Va.
Population Genetics	8/2-8/6	Miami, Fla.
Advanced Crime Mapping	8/9-8/13	Brookline, Mass.
Forensic Microscopy	8/16-8/20	Chicago, Ill.
Basic Training in Medicolegal Death Investigation	9/13-9/17	New York, N.Y.

For more information on the above courses or to view a complete list of upcoming NIJ sponsored trainings, go to: http://www.ojp.usdoj.gov/nij/training/welcome.htm.

Newest Research Findings

Helping Ideas Travel

Last year NIJ's International Center created a new product line: transferability assessments. Transferability assessments identify innovative programs and technologies around the world and assess whether these innovations could be adapted for American justice systems. They ask a series of investigative questions about the nature of the innovation, laws, resources and structural factors that help its operation, performance data, and cultural influences.

Three transferability assessments have been completed so far.

One is a European Union public-private partnership between law enforcement, civic organizations and Internet service providers to combat Internet child exploitation. Tip lines identify possible child pornography sites, and investigators and service providers collaborate to verify and shut them down.

Another examined a "virtual autopsy" that performs noninvasive death investigations. By using a combination of MRIs, CT scans and body surface scans, examiners can complete many autopsies in less time and for less money.

The third examined the potential that European and Latin American income-based "day" fines have for reducing American correctional populations. Day fines could be used as criminal sanctions for a wide range of offenses. They could also be an alternative sanction to probation and parole revocations.

▶ Read more: http://www.ncjrs.gov/pdffiles1/nij/grants/230400.pdf;
  http://www.ncjrs.gov/pdffiles1/nij/grants/230401.pdf.

Crime During the Transition to Adulthood

The transition to adulthood is a complex period for all youth, but it may be increasingly more difficult for youth "aging out" of the child welfare system. Foster youth aging out of the welfare system lose the system's support when they reach a certain age; a period when their risk for engagement in crime increases dramatically.

Crime During the Transition to Adulthood: How Youth Fare as They Leave Out-of-Home Care, a final report submitted to NIJ, examines criminal behavior and criminal justice system involvement among youth transitioning from the child welfare system to independent adulthood. Using data from the Midwest Study of the Adult Functioning of Former Foster Youth, researchers found that offending trends among aging-out youth are similar to those seen in the general population. Findings also show that higher numbers of foster care placements correspond with increases in both violent and nonviolent crime.

▶ Read more: http://www.ncjrs.gov/pdffiles1/nij/grants/229666.pdf.

Go to the NIJ Web site at http://www.ojp.usdoj.dov/nij and subscribe to our e-mail alerts to receive the latest information on funding, publications, trainings, events and topical pages.

.gov

See the NIJ Web site for multimedia links throughout this issue and look for the following online content:

▶ The new NIJ International Center Web page

▶ David Weisburd discussing hot spots policing

▶ Dennis Rosenbaum discussing the policing life cycle

▶ David Olds discussing the long-term effects of nurse visits on criminal behavior

▶ Larry Sherman discussing how states can reduce crime by reallocating spending

▶ New and updated Web pages on:

  • Hot spots policing

  • Hawaii HOPE

  • Roadside safety

▶ NIJ funding opportunities and awards

▶ The online archive of back issues of the *NIJ Journal*

http://www.ojp.usdoj.gov/nij

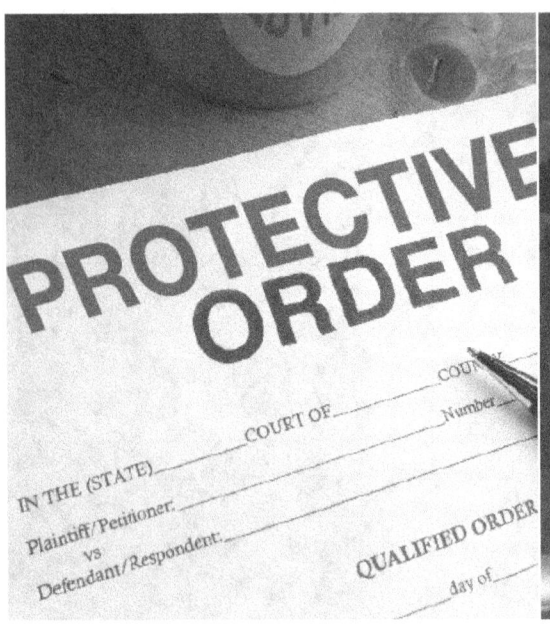

Perspectives on Civil Protective Orders in Domestic Violence Cases: The Rural and Urban Divide

by Nikki Hawkins

Civil protective orders can be an effective tool for domestic violence prevention.

Subtle jurisdictional differences influence how women experience civil protective orders.

A recent study looked at the impact of civil protective orders for domestic violence victims in five Kentucky jurisdictions. Civil protective orders, sometimes known as restraining orders, may cover various situations, such as ordering an assailant to avoid a victim's home and workplace or forbidding any contact with the victim, including by mail or telephone. Findings from the study suggest that orders make a difference in safety, fear levels and cost savings. Moreover, urban and rural populations reported significant differences in fear. Half of the women who received protective orders did not experience a violation within the following six months. For the half

who did experience violations, the levels of violence and abuse declined significantly compared with the six months before the protective order was issued.

Urban and rural women had similar views of the protective orders' effectiveness. However, rural women found more barriers to getting an order and having it enforced, thus experiencing less relief from fear and abuse. The study also explored the role of stalking in protective order violations and quantified the overall cost to society.

Teri Faragher, co-author of the report and executive director of the Domestic Violence Prevention Board in Lexington, Ky., said the findings would provide important information for practitioners. She said that knowing their interventions matter would make a difference for judges and prosecutors.

Fear of Future Harm

Researchers interviewed 213 women with protective orders in one urban and four rural jurisdictions. T.K. Logan of the University of Kentucky, the lead researcher, noted that the rural women were from the Appalachian area, which has received media attention because of drug use. This attention may have affected community differences such as law enforcement priorities if some agencies were focusing more on drug use than on domestic violence.

One significant finding is that, overall, rural women were more afraid of future harm than their urban counterparts. Participants rated the degree to which they feared future harm in various categories on a scale ranging from "not at all fearful" to "extremely fearful." More rural women were somewhat or extremely fearful in every category during the baseline interview and at the six-month follow-up. Six months after they were first interviewed, both rural

> The study's findings would provide important information for practitioners. Knowing their interventions matter would make a difference for judges and prosecutors.

and urban women reported that they felt less fearful once they got the protective orders. The chart below shows the percentage of women who reported being somewhat or extremely afraid of future harm by type of fear.

Factors such as isolation and fewer community services may contribute to higher fear levels for women in rural areas, and some fundamental differences between urban and rural women may also play a role. For example, the study found that rural women were more entrenched in their relationships. More rural women were or had been married to the men named in the protective orders.

On average, they had been in their relationships longer and were more likely to have children in common with the men than their urban counterparts.

The study focused only on women who got protective orders and therefore cannot provide comparable data about women who did not seek or were denied protective orders. Consequently, it is not clear if the declines in violations and fear levels are a result of the protective orders, another factor or some combination of factors. Women who are more seriously injured or fearful may be more likely to seek protective orders than those who feel less threatened.

Barriers to Getting a Protective Order

To learn about the barriers to getting a protective order and their effects on rural and urban women, Logan interviewed 188 key participants, including judges, law enforcement officers, prosecutors, defense attorneys and court clerks. Other participants included victim services workers, such as advocates, legal aid attorneys, shelter staff and counselors.

Women Reporting They Are Somewhat or Extremely Fearful of Future Harm

Type of fear	Rural (n = 93)		Urban (n = 77)	
	At baseline (shortly after receiving order)	Six months after receiving order	At baseline (shortly after receiving order)	Six months after receiving order
Threats and harassment	80%	61%	67%	41%
Physical injury	65%	46%	43%	26%
Control	74%	53%	57%	32%
Humiliation	84%	55%	59%	37%
Financial	74%	48%	59%	21%
Child interference or harm	82%	59%	52%	34%
Hurt others	75%	49%	33%	29%

Participants were asked three main questions: What do you think are the three biggest barriers in your community to obtaining a protective order? What do you think are the three main reasons a woman might not receive an emergency protective order? What are the three biggest reasons a judge would dismiss or not grant a domestic violence order?

Forty percent of participants mentioned "judicial bias" as a barrier to obtaining a protective order. Judicial bias may include the judge's personal political connections to the families involved or the history of protective order requests if a woman has filed multiple times. Judicial bias was mentioned as a barrier more often in the rural areas than in the urban areas.

In fact, rural respondents reported political barriers throughout the protective order process, saying that "who you know" and the "good ol' boy" network factored into the experience.

Kentucky Circuit Family Court Judge Jo Ann Wise said she was not surprised that judicial bias surfaced as a barrier, especially for rural women. "I've heard judicial bias myself. It's there," she said.

Urban women reported having trouble navigating the system, even though they reported it took (on average) one and a half hours to get their protective orders, compared with the two and half hours it took rural women. They also reported experiencing more confusion, encountering more problems and having more questions about the process than rural women. Urban women also expressed more fear of confronting their violent partners in court.

Stalking: A Looming Risk

In prior research, Logan found that about half of the victims who get protective orders are stalked.[1] Overall, protective orders were less effective for stalking victims than for other victims. Specifically:

- Women who were stalked by their violent partner before getting a protective order had a strong likelihood of protective order violations.

> Stalking victims experienced higher distress levels and more property loss, lost more sleep, and took more time off from work, contributing to higher societal costs.

- Women who were stalked after the protective order were more afraid of future harm, experienced more distress related to the abuse, and endured more violence and more property damage.
- Women who were stalked after the protective order felt the order to be less effective compared with those who were not stalked.
- Stalking after the protective order was associated with violence, suggesting those who stalk are more violent and more resistant to court intervention.

The previous study examined victims with no protective order violations, victims whose protective orders were violated, and victims with violations and stalking. Stalking victims experienced higher distress levels and more property loss, lost more sleep, and took more time off from work, contributing to higher societal costs.

"I think that with stalkers we are dealing with a different kind of offender," Logan said. "This type of offender is costing the system all the way around. More assertively addressing stalking would save society more and help more victims. That's what the data point to."

Stalking victims were less likely than other women to report a protective order violation. They said they felt the complaint would not be taken seriously or they feared they did not have enough proof.

Faragher explained how her community is addressing stalking. In 2006, Faragher's Domestic Violence Prevention Board received an arrest and enforcement grant from the Department of Justice's Office on Violence Against Women and launched several domestic violence prevention programs. For example, in the Lexington-Fayette County police department, a police sergeant has been assigned to review all domestic violence reports. If the sergeant identifies stalking behaviors in a report that did not result in a stalking charge, the sergeant assigns the case to a domestic violence detective for further investigation. In addition, the sergeant uses the review as a training tool to provide information to patrol officers on how to intervene more effectively in cases involving stalking.

Wise said victims may not use the word "stalking," but the behavior is obvious in her courtroom.

Research in Practice: When a Researcher-Practitioner Partnership Works

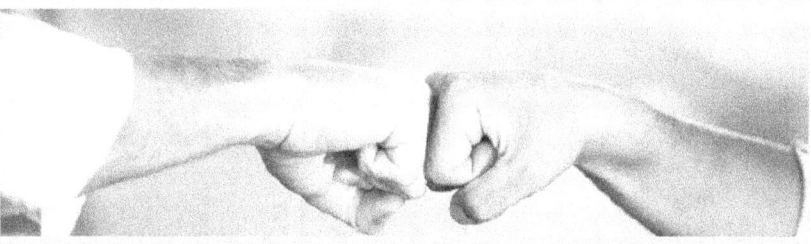

An effective researcher-practitioner relationship can produce many benefits, but perhaps the most marked result from the Kentucky civil protective order study was the immediate use of the research findings to improve criminal justice system responses to stalking cases.

Researcher T.K. Logan conducted interviews with 213 women who received protective orders. Among other questions, Logan asked what obstacles participants had experienced. Nearly a quarter of the reported barriers to getting protective orders were "clerks/gatekeeper attitudes." Logan consulted co-author Teri Faragher, executive director of the Domestic Violence Prevention Board in Lexington, Ky., and learned that she had been hearing similar reports. Armed with concrete data, Faragher could address the problem more effectively.

"Because T.K. found that a large number of women were having similar experiences," Faragher said, "it wasn't just anecdotal anymore. Whether it was language barriers or simply being turned away, there were a lot of similar reports. Because these problems were called out and identified, things have improved tremendously already. There is a long-term effort in place to correct barriers for women getting protective orders now."

One of Logan's main goals is to have her research make a difference to the community. Including the practitioner's perspective from the onset is one way for Logan to achieve that goal.

"I have a strong belief: Why do research if nobody is going to use it?" Logan said. "By working with practitioners, it's upping my chances that my research will be useful. I am not in the trenches, not on the front lines. They help me think about things I didn't think about. Or give me an alternative explanation I didn't consider. If you really want your research to make a difference, it increases the chances for that to happen."

Faragher said Logan's empathetic interviewing techniques help obtain useful information.

"T.K. likes to work with people in the field," Faragher said. "Her interests involve more than just the empirical findings; she wants to know how the systems work. We might say there's a 24-hour hotline available for victims, but when she talks to them, they tell her the reality — 'well yes, there's a hotline, but when I called it I got an answering machine.' The way she conducts her interviews and gathers information provides invaluable feedback for the systems and the way they work."

Logan and Faragher first worked together in 2002 when they examined custody and visitation issues related to domestic violence. Faragher said Logan's research helped to redirect her group's advocacy efforts. Since then, their relationship has grown, much to the benefit of the research.

"With T.K., we have these two perspectives, and when we bring them together it's symbiotic," Faragher said. "But that requires discussion. To get to that place of agreement, there has to be a lot of discussion. For example, we talk about interventions a lot — what the next steps need to be after the research. We have developed a strong enough working relationship that can withstand open discussion and disagreement."

To see a video of Logan and Faragher discussing the researcher and practitioner relationship, go to http://www.ojp.usdoj.gov/nij/journals/media.htm.

"Stalking has changed the way I look at petitions," Wise said. "Stalking has always been a factor, but before these studies I didn't realize how much stalking affected victims. Now when I'm reading petitions I make a note of stalking behaviors. Big ones I see are 'He followed me to work. When I came out of work, he was at my car.' Or 'I've seen him driving by the house.' It's a serious factor I need to consider. There's such a strong connection to lethality."

Every January, the Department of Justice and the National Center for Victims of Crime promote National Stalking Awareness Month to educate the public and professionals about the dangers of stalking. The "Stalking Fact Sheet"[2] shows that 76 percent of females murdered in domestic violence incidents were stalked before they were killed and 54 percent reported stalking to the police before their deaths — statistics that support Logan's findings and Wise's concerns.

The Cost of Abuse and the Cost of Protective Orders

In collaboration with economist William Hoyt, Logan calculated the costs and benefits of protective orders — a useful measure in economically difficult times and one that few intervention studies consider.

According to the study, every dollar spent on the protective order intervention produced $30.75 in avoided costs to society. The state of Kentucky saved about $85 million over a one-year period because of significant declines in abuse and violence.

The savings included "relevant costs," such as service use, legal system use, lost opportunities and quality of life loss. Participants were asked to recall events during the six months before the study started and record information for six months after the protective order was issued. Participants included data about services (health services, mental health services, shelter and advocacy) used because of the abuse, time lost from work and other activities, and mileage and property losses stemming from the abuse. In addition, the women were asked to record the distress they experienced from the abuse for each month. A dollar amount was assigned to each factor, providing the basis for the analysis.

"The numbers are staggering," said Wise. "When she [Logan] broke it down to the cost benefit of having a protective order — it's amazing to see how much money we could save … right now in this economy, saving money and financial impact is something everyone wants to talk about."

Although the study suggests that protective orders may be an effective tool for domestic violence prevention, it also suggests that more work is necessary for women to feel better protected. Specifically, the study suggests the following areas for improvement:

- Encourage full use and enforcement when violations occur.
- Develop more effective interventions to address stalking at all levels (all community agencies need to pay more attention to stalking as a risk factor).
- Address barriers to service access and enforcement.

"In family court, follow-up studies are invaluable to us," Wise said. "If we're not doing something effective, we want to know."

The National Institute of Justice funded the study. The complete report is available at http://www.ncjrs.gov/pdffiles1/nij/grants/228350.pdf.

Nikki Hawkins is a communications associate with Palladian Partners Inc. She is a former police officer for the city of Rockville, Md.

NCJ 230410

Notes

1. Logan, T.K., L. Shannon, and J. Cole. "Stalking Victimization in the Context of Intimate Partner Violence," *Violence and Victims* 22 (6) (2007): 679.

2. http://www.stalkingawarenessmonth.org/sites/default/files/2010/Stalking%20Fact%20Sheet%202009_ENG_color.PDF

Visit NIJ's Web topic page on domestic violence issues at http://www.ojp.usdoj.gov/nij/topics/crime/intimate-partner-violence.

To watch T.K. Logan's presentation of her findings to the National Council of Juvenile and Family Court Judges, as well as an interview with Logan, go to http://www.ojp.usdoj.gov/nij/journals/media.htm.

The National Institute of Justice Commemorates the 15th Anniversary of the Violence Against Women Act

n 1994, the U.S. Congress enacted the Violence Against Women Act, a comprehensive legislative package that marked the first major investment by the federal government in state and local efforts to address violence against women. VAWA recognized the devastating consequences that violence has on women, families and society as a whole. VAWA also acknowledged that violence against women requires specialized responses to address unique barriers that prevent victims from seeking assistance from the justice system.

The Violence Against Women and Department of Justice Reauthorization Act of 2005 (VAWA 2005) further improved legal tools and grant programs addressing domestic violence, dating violence, sexual assault and stalking. With the help of VAWA funding, NIJ has sponsored several research grants whose findings have further illustrated the challenges and potential solutions to ending these crimes.

NIJ proudly joins the Office on Violence Against Women in commemorating 15 years of working together to end gender-based violence.

The following NIJ-sponsored research reports relevant to violence against women can be found on the NCJRS Web site:

■ Practical Implications of Current Domestic Violence Research: For Law Enforcement, Prosecutors and Judges

http://www.ncjrs.gov/pdffiles1/nij/225722.pdf

■ Extent, Nature, and Consequences of Rape Victimization: Findings From the National Violence Against Women Survey

http://www.ncjrs.gov/pdffiles1/nij/210346.pdf

■ Research Results From a National Study of Intimate Partner Homicide: The Danger Assessment Instrument (From Violence Against Women and Family Violence: Developments in Research, Practice, and Policy)

http://www.ncjrs.gov/pdffiles1/nij/199710.pdf

■ Systems Change Analysis of SANE Programs: Identifying the Mediating Mechanisms of Criminal Justice System Impact: Project Summary

http://www.ncjrs.gov/pdffiles1/nij/grants/226498.pdf

■ The Sexual Victimization of College Women

http://www.ncjrs.gov/pdffiles1/nij/182369.pdf

■ The Campus Sexual Assault (CSA) Study

http://www.ncjrs.gov/pdffiles1/nij/grants/221153.pdf

■ Stalking: Its Role in Serious Domestic Violence Cases

http://www.ncjrs.gov/pdffiles1/nij/grants/187346.pdf

NCJ 230411

Visit NIJ's Web topic page on violence against women and family violence programs at http://www.ojp.usdoj.gov/nij/topics/crime/violence-against-women/welcome.htm

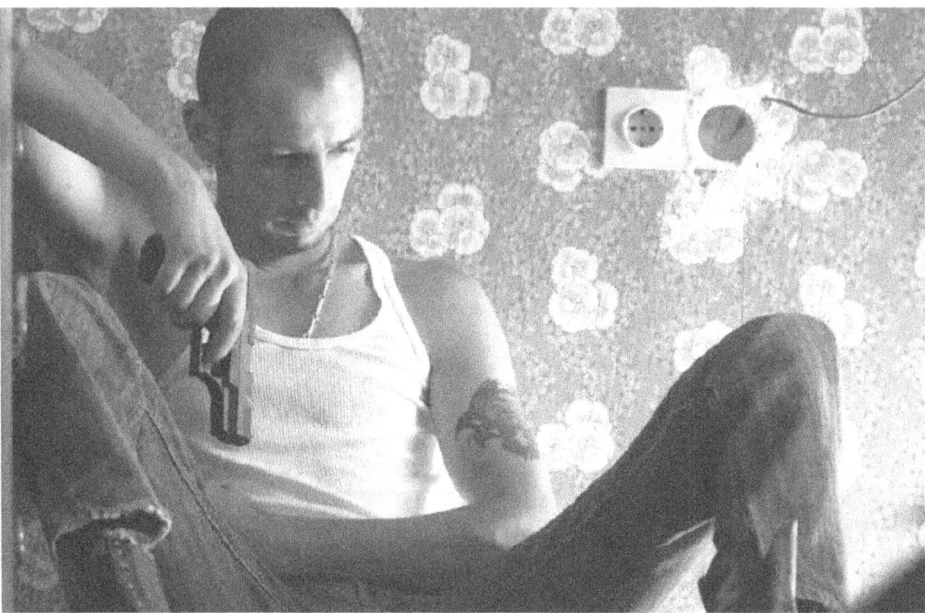

Men Who Murder Their Families: What the Research Tells Us

by Bernie Auchter

NIJ hosts a forum to discuss the problem and the warning signs that foreshadow these events.

Cases where people kill their families and then commit suicide are mercifully rare.

Less extreme forms of domestic violence and child abuse are more common. Acts of partner conflict can fall on a broad spectrum, ranging from verbal criticisms to cases of a family homicide followed by suicide. The research identifies several risk factors that may indeed predict more severe domestic violence cases.

In a seminar titled Men Who Murder Their Families: What the Research Tells Us, an expert panel discussed a recent spike in news reports of "familicide" cases. Panelists included Jacquelyn C. Campbell of Johns Hopkins University, author David Adams, and Richard Gelles of the University of Pennsylvania.

Campbell, Anna D. Wolf Chair and professor at JHU's School of Nursing, discussed the Centers for Disease Control and Prevention's National Violent Death Reporting System. Of the 408 homicide-suicide cases, most perpetrators were men (91 percent) and most used a gun (88 percent). A 12-city study that Campbell conducted of these cases found that intimate-partner violence had previously occurred in 70 percent of them. Interestingly, only 25 percent of prior domestic violence appeared in the arrest records, according to Campbell. Researchers uncovered much of the prior domestic violence through interviews with family and friends of the homicide victims. "Prior domestic violence is by far the number-one risk factor in these cases," Campbell said.

She also explained that most people who commit murder-suicide are non-Hispanic white males who kill their mates or former mates. Prior domestic violence is the greatest risk factor in these cases. Access to a gun is a significant risk factor, as are threats with a weapon, a step-child in the home or estrangement. However, a past criminal history is not a reliable or significant predictor in murder-suicide.

In the aftermath of a family murder followed by a suicide, communities, police, researchers and others search for explanations. In difficult finan-cial times, it may be natural to look for economic influences, especially when the killer has recently lost a job or has enormous financial problems. Campbell found that unemployment was a significant risk factor for murder-suicide but only when combined with a history of domestic violence. In other words, it was not a risk factor in and of itself but was something that tipped the scale following previous abuse.

Adams, author of *Why Do They Kill? Men Who Murder Their Intimate Partners,* offered his perspective based on years of research and experience working with domes-tic violence cases. His comments focused mostly on guns and jealousy in these violent crimes. When we consider prevention, guns are essen-tially the "low-hanging fruit," he suggested. He cited research, similar to Campbell's data, showing that 92 percent of murder-suicides involved a gun in a sample of 591 cases. Adams

> Ninety percent of the time the best predictor of domestic violence is past behavior.

compared high rates of intimate-partner homicide in the United States with the considerably lower rates in other wealthy countries. He noted that America has the most permis-sive gun laws of any industrialized nation. He made a similar compar-ison among U.S. states that have restrictive versus permissive gun laws and lower versus higher homi-cide and suicide rates. Three reasons guns are used frequently is that they are more efficient than other weap-ons, can be used impulsively, and can be used to terrorize and threaten.

In the research for his book, Adams asked those who killed with guns if they would have used another weapon if a gun were not available; most said no.

"The most common type of killer was a possessively jealous type, and I found that many of the men who … commit murder-suicide, as well as those who kill their children, also seem to fit that profile," Adams said. "A jealous substance abuser with a gun poses a particularly deadly com-bination of factors; one that was present in about 40 percent of the killers I interviewed," he added.

Gelles, professor and dean of the School of Social Policy & Practice at the University of Pennsylvania, said that 90 percent of the time the best predictor of domestic violence is past behavior. He said the proxi-mate social and demographic factors that are related to all forms of fam-ily violence except sexual abuse are

poverty, unemployment and family stressors, which include disagree-ments over money, sex and children. The economy always is a distal factor that is translated into family relations through poverty or employment or self-image or stressors.

Recent economic problems may produce increases in child abuse and neglect and domestic violence. In the subset of men who kill their entire families, there is a small increase in atypical familicide. These atypical cases are not the posses-sive, controlling husbands with guns. The familicides that are represented by men who kill their wives, their children and themselves are what the famous French sociologist Emile Durkheim called "anomic suicides." These occur when there are radical and significant changes in the person's social and economic environment.

The United States experienced economic disruptions in 2001 and in the recession of 1990. However, they did not produce huge waves of violence, either in child abuse or domestic violence, Gelles said. Anomic suicide "is not suicide because you've lost all your money but suicide because the rules of the game have changed — because what you thought would be true about your life and your family and your 401(k) and the loyalty of your company has suddenly been dis-rupted," he said. Gelles suggested that this difficult disruption mixed with an "overenmeshment" in one's family could underlie these familicides.

Overenmeshment is a condition in which perpetrators either view "their family members as posses-sions that they control or [they] don't see any boundaries between their identity, their wife and their children. And so these are suicides of the entire family, where the anomic, overly enmeshed individual can't bear to leave the pain behind and so takes his wife and children with him," he said.

If the familicide cases signal a more general increase in domestic violence, one result could be a dramatic increase in child abuse and a subsequent burden on the foster care system, Gelles said.

The discussion also touched on new concerns, such as how abusers use threats to intimidate. The panelists focused on the point of separation as a vulnerable period.

Bernie Auchter is a senior social science analyst with the Violence and Victimization Research Division at NIJ.

NCJ 230412

Visit the NIJ Web page, "Murder-Suicide in Families," to watch or listen to the seminar or to read the transcript: http://www.ojp.usdoj.gov/nij/topics/crime/intimate-partner-violence/murder-suicide.htm.

Are You Interested in Becoming …
a Peer Reviewer for the National Institute of Justice?

NIJ is seeking reviewers to assess grant applications in FY 2010. The Institute needs reviewers from diverse backgrounds and regions who have relevant expertise and experience in at least one of the following areas:

- Crime control and prevention research.

- Criminology, law enforcement or corrections.

- DNA analysis, research and development.

- Information and sensor technologies.

- Investigative and forensic science and technology.

- Justice systems research.

- Law enforcement technologies.

- Violence and victimization research.

Some reviews are conducted remotely, whereas others involve in-person meetings. Reviewers score 10 to 15 applications within a two-to-four-week period. Before beginning their work, reviewers must participate in an orientation telephone call, which covers the role and responsibilities of the reviewers and the background and purpose of the grant program under review. Participants receive $125 for each application reviewed.

If you are interested in becoming a peer reviewer, please send an up-to-date resume or curriculum vitae, including a valid e-mail address, to Sherran Thomas at sherran.thomas@usdoj.gov or Jami Freitag at jamissen.freitag@usdoj.gov.

Stalking resource center
2000 ~ A DECADE OF ~ 2010
AWARENESS ACTION ADVOCACY

Voices From the Field: Stalking

by Michelle M. Garcia

Stalking often goes undetected, so how can the victims be protected?

S talking is common, dangerous, and — far too often — lethal.

A seminal 2009 Bureau of Justice Statistics report showed that stalkers victimize 3.4 million people each year in the United States.[1] Both males and females can be victims of stalking, but females are nearly three times as likely to be stalking victims.[2]

Domestic violence-related stalking is the most common type of stalking and the most dangerous. Nearly 75 percent of stalking victims know their stalker in some way; in about 30 percent of cases, the stalker is a current or former intimate partner.[3] The 1998 National Violence Against Women Survey found that more than three-fourths of the female victims of intimate partner stalking reported physical assaults by that partner and one-third reported sexual assaults.[4]

Stalkers who are former intimate partners have considerable leverage over their victims because they know a great deal about them. They are more insulting, interfering and threatening than non-intimate partner stalkers.[5] Such stalkers are likely to know the victims' friends or family members as well as where the victims work, shop and go for entertainment. This knowledge provides potentially endless opportunities for stalkers to terrorize victims.

If there are children in common, the victim may find it impossible to avoid all contact with the stalker. In fact, through continuing court dates or court-ordered visits, the legal system often unintentionally enables stalkers to gain access to the victims or to continue harassing and intimidating them. Intimate partners are more likely to approach victims physically, to use weapons and to reoffend, and their behaviors are more likely to intensify quickly.[6]

Most alarmingly, stalking can be lethal. According to one study, 76 percent of women who were murdered by their current or former intimate partners were stalked by their killers within 12 months of the murder.[7] The same study found that 85 percent of women who were victims of attempted homicide by their current or former intimate partners were stalked within 12 months before the attempted murder. Despite what research shows and headlines tragically report, stalking is frequently undetected and misunderstood, and its seriousness is often minimized.

Why Stalking May Not Be Viewed as Seriously as Other Crimes

Offender behaviors such as making repeated phone calls, continually driving by a victim's house, leaving unwanted gifts or letters, and showing up unexpectedly are frequently not identified as stalking by either criminal justice responders or victims. Only about half of victims who experience unwanted or harassing contacts identify their experience as stalking.[8] Yet, under the laws of all 50 states, when these independent and seemingly benign behaviors

become a pattern, the result is the crime of stalking. When the stalker also commits domestic violence, investigations are likely to focus on the violence rather than the stalking. In comparison with acts of physical violence, stalking may seem less significant, and the dangers represented by stalking may be overlooked.

This seeming lack of recognition may be in part because stalking is still a new crime. Only within the past two decades has the criminal justice system held stalkers accountable and become aware that stalking victims are in great danger. California passed the first stalking law in 1990. By 1999, all states and the District of Columbia had passed laws criminalizing stalking. Yet criminal justice practitioners receive little or no stalking training, and staff members of domestic violence and sexual assault programs often lack a clear understanding of the interrelationship between stalking and other crimes.

Social Norms

Victims, offenders and those who work with both are influenced by social messages that minimize the seriousness of stalking. Films often portray stalking as romantic (for example, *High Fidelity* and *St. Elmo's Fire*), comedic (for example, *All About Steve* and *The Cable Guy*), or both as in the film *There's*

Something About Mary. Across styles of music, songs romanticize or out-and-out promote stalking. In recent years, a major national retailer stocked a t-shirt that read, "Some call it stalking, I call it love." Only after significant and repeated public outcries did the retailer remove the shirt from its shelves. But many other retailers continue to sell such messages. Typing "stalking t-shirt" into a search engine yields dozens of variations on the message that stalking is not a big deal.

Next Steps

Clearly, much work still needs to be done in the United States to increase awareness of the realities of stalking. As long as an alarming number of people are victimized every year, we must do more to keep victims safe and hold offenders accountable. Each of us can begin by assessing our own community's understanding of stalking and working to improve our responses to this serious crime.

Michelle M. Garcia is the director of the Stalking Resource Center of the National Center for Victims of Crime.

NCJ 230413

Notes

1. Baum, K., S. Catalano, M. Rand, and K. Rose, *Stalking Victimization in the United States*, Special Report, Washington, DC: U.S. Department of Justice, Bureau of Justice Statistics, January 2009, NCJ 224527, http://bjs.ojp.usdoj.gov/content/pub/pdf/svus.pdf.

2. Ibid.

3. Ibid.

4. Tjaden, P., and K. Thoennes, *Stalking in America: Findings From the National Violence Against Women Survey*, Research in Brief, Washington, DC:

U.S. Department of Justice, National Institute of Justice, and Centers for Disease Control and Prevention, April 1998, NCJ 169592, http://www.ncjrs.gov/pdffiles/169592.pdf.

5. Mohandie, K., R. Meloy, M. Green McGowan, and J. Williams, "The RECON Typology of Stalking: Reliability and Validity Based Upon a Large Sample of North American Stalkers," *Journal of Forensic Sciences* 51 (1) (January 2006): 147-155.

6. Ibid.

7. McFarlane, J.M., J.C. Campbell, S. Wilt, C.J. Sachs, Y. Ulrich, and X. Xu, "Stalking and Intimate Partner Femicide," *Homicide Studies* 3 (4) (1999): 311.

8. Baum, K., *Stalking Victimization in the United States*.

 **www.** *Visit NIJ's Web topic page on stalking at http://www.ojp.usdoj.gov/nij/topics/crime/stalking/welcome.htm and at the Stalking Resource Center at http://www.ncvc.org/src.*

Predictive Policing: The Future of Law Enforcement?

by Beth Pearsall

Law enforcement explores ways to anticipate and prevent crime.

For years, businesses have used data analysis to anticipate market conditions or industry trends and drive sales strategies.

Walmart, for example, learned through analysis that when a major weather event is in the forecast, demand for three items rises: duct tape, bottled water and strawberry Pop-Tarts. Armed with this information, stores in the affected areas can ensure their shelves are fully stocked to meet customer needs.

Police can use a similar data analysis to help make their work more efficient. The idea is being called "predictive policing," and some in the field believe it has the potential to transform law enforcement by enabling police to anticipate and prevent crime instead of simply responding to it.

In November 2009, the National Institute of Justice, in partnership with the Bureau of Justice Assistance and the Los Angeles Police Department, held a Predictive Policing Symposium to discuss this emerging idea and its impact on the future of policing. Researchers, law enforcement officers, crime analysts and scientists gathered in Los Angeles for three days to explore the policy implications, privacy issues and technology of predictive policing.

What Is Predictive Policing?

Predictive policing, in essence, is taking data from disparate sources, analyzing them and then using results to anticipate, prevent and respond more effectively to future crime.

Predictive policing entails becoming less reactive. "The predictive vision moves law enforcement from focusing on what happened to focusing on what will happen and how to effectively deploy resources in front of crime, thereby changing outcomes," writes Charlie Beck, chief of the Los Angeles Police Department.[1]

Beck told participants that perhaps the greatest benefit to predictive policing is the discovery of new or previously unknown patterns and trends. Just as Walmart found increased demand for strawberry Pop-Tarts preceding major weather events, LAPD has found its own subtle patterns when examining data that have helped the department accurately anticipate and prevent crime.

Predictive policing is not meant to replace tried-and-true police techniques, symposium speakers explained. Instead, it borrows from the principles of problem-oriented policing, community policing, evidence-based policing, intelligence-led policing and other proven policing models.

"This is a very important next step to move forward in the evolutionary process of our profession," said Bill Bratton, former LAPD chief and chairman of Altegrity Risk International. "We are building on the essential elements of all policing strategies for the greater good."

John Morgan, director of NIJ's Office of Science and Technology, added, "This is a framework to help us organize policing as an information-intensive business in an information age. Predictive policing is not meant to replace any other model of policing," he said. "Instead, it enables us to do these things better."

Moreover, doing them better remains critical given the current economic climate.

George Gascón, chief of police for the San Francisco Police Department, noted that predictive policing is the perfect tool to help departments become more efficient as budgets continue to be reduced. "With predictive policing, we have the tools to put cops at the right place at the right time or bring other services to impact crime, and we can do so with less," he said.

> Predictive policing is not meant to replace tried-and-true police techniques. It builds on the essential elements of all policing strategies for the greater good.

So What Does It Look Like in the Field?

"There is no predictive policing in a box," explained Colleen McCue, president and CEO of MC² Solutions, which provides professional services in predictive analytics. "Let the problem guide the solution," she advised.

Current analytic tools and techniques like hot spots, data mining, crime mapping, geospatial prediction and social network analysis can be applied to a broad range of criminal justice problems. For instance, they can be used to anticipate localized crime spikes, inform city and neighborhood planning, and aid in police management decisions.

Here are two examples of predictive policing at work:

Reducing Random Gunfire in Richmond. Every New Year's Eve, Richmond, Va., would experience an increase in random gunfire. Police began looking at data gathered over the years, and based on that information, they were able to anticipate the time, location and nature of future incidents. On New Year's Eve 2003, Richmond police placed officers at those locations to prevent crime and respond more rapidly. The result was a 47 percent decrease in random gunfire and a 246 percent increase in weapons seized. The department saved $15,000 in personnel costs.

Connecting Burglaries and Code Violations in Arlington, Texas. The Arlington, Texas, Police Department used data on residential burglaries to identify hot spots and then compared these locations to areas with code violations. According to Chief Theron Bowman, officers found that every unit increase of physical decay resulted in almost six more residential burglaries in the city. Thus, neighborhoods with greater physical decay could expect greater increases in residential burglaries. Arlington subsequently developed a formula to help identify characteristics of these "fragile neighborhoods." The police department and other city agencies now work more efficiently in the neighborhoods to help prevent crime.

But Is This New?

Some participants questioned whether predictive policing was, in fact, a new model. They argued that good crime analysts have been practicing predictive policing for more than 40 years.

"Are we doing anything new or innovative with this data or are we just doing it better and quicker?" asked Chief Tom Casady of the Lincoln, Neb., Police Department.

Casady argued that the idea is not new. "It is a coalescing of interrelated police strategies and tactics that were already around, like intelligence-led policing and problem solving. This just brings them all under the umbrella of predictive policing," he said. "What is new is the tremendous infusion of data," Casady added.

Referencing the Richmond example, he explained, "We knew there were shootings on New Year's Eve, and we knew where they were happening. So if we could pinpoint the time, we could put more police in those areas. This is pretty basic stuff," he said, "and we have been doing this for years." Casady said the real question the field should be asking is how to take this to a new level: How do we use information to stimulate different interventions?

Community Involvement Is Critical

Participants agreed that transparency and community involvement are important.

"Community trust is huge as we move down this path," Beck explained. "We need to be extremely transparent. As we advance this discussion of how law enforcement will use information and how we tie that information to officer deployment, all of these discussions must be open."

"The community must have confidence that law enforcement will

NIJ Funds Predictive Policing Demonstration Initiative

NIJ has launched a demonstration initiative to develop, test and evaluate predictive policing in a real-world, real-time context. The Institute awarded planning grants to seven law enforcement agencies.

NIJ has also funded a team from the RAND Corp. to evaluate the projects. The evaluation is designed to address questions such as what works, what does not and what is promising in predictive policing.

For more information on the initiative, see http://www.ojp.usdoj.gov/nij/topics/law-enforcement/predictive-policing/symposium/discussion-demonstrations.htm.

handle information the right way," said Thomas O'Reilly, senior policy advisor at the justice department's Bureau of Justice Assistance. "As we move into predictive policing, nothing should be secret. We should engage privacy advocates and community leaders from the outset to explain the program and get their ideas and input to alleviate their concerns."

Sean Malinowski, a lieutenant with the LAPD, assured participants that predictive policing does not deny civil rights. "Police are not arresting people on the probability that they will commit a crime," he said. "Police still must have probable cause." In addition, predictive policing methods do not identify specific individuals; instead, they anticipate particular times and locations where crime is likely to occur.[2]

Yet privacy and civil liberty issues are critically interrelated with predictive policing and must be addressed. "We have a solemn obligation and a strategic imperative for the success of predictive

policing to put privacy, civil rights and civil liberties in the forefront from the outset," said Russell Porter, director of the State of Iowa Intelligence Fusion Center.

Participants stressed the importance of setting up a thorough privacy policy, training personnel to use it properly, enforcing accountability and continually refining the policy. Policies should also include what information can be shared with other agencies.

"Transparency, auditing and due diligence are critical to developing a process that is trustworthy, protects privacy and produces good outcomes," said Joan McNamara, a commander in the Los Angeles Police Department.

Bratton added, "If we do this right, if we do it constitutionally, collectively and transparently, we can lessen the concern. We can hear the concerns and move forward, all the while expanding and modifying and improving and continuing that path of discussion."

It Is All About the Data

In the end, the success of predictive policing will all come down to how reliable it is, how different information sources are integrated and how all the data are analyzed.

"Police departments collect great data all the time," said Craig Uchida, president of Justice & Security Strategies Inc, a company that helps law enforcement agencies in evaluating and addressing program needs. "We just don't know how reliable, valid and clean it is. We need to oversee data collection to ensure the data are clean."

Along with watching quality, police departments also need to tap into the wealth of nontraditional data available locally, such as medical and code-compliance data.

"Predictive policing has another level outside the walls of the police department," Jim Bueermann, chief of police in the Redlands, Calif., Police Department, said. "It takes a holistic approach — how do we integrate health and school and land-use data?"

"Part of the challenge is understanding what all the available data are and then finding a way to fuse that data, bring the people who use that data together, and approach it from a holistic perspective," Bowman said. "It is just as important to understand what we don't know at the local level."

John Miller of the Office of the Director of National Intelligence suggested that the field also looks at "predictive perpetrating." "We must ask ourselves: What data sources have the bad guys pulled up? We are not the only ones looking at data," he warned.

"It is so important to bring these data warehouses and analytics together and to search and make them available so we can do our job," Beck said. Malinowski added, "Analyzing all of this data will give decision-makers better information to make better decisions."

"We have the ability to use information to save lives, and we need to use it constitutionally and consistently," Bratton said. "We are in a position to save lives, reduce injuries, improve safety ... It doesn't get any better than that."

Beth Pearsall is a freelance writer and frequent contributor to the *NIJ Journal*.

NCJ 230414

"We have the ability to use information to save lives, and we need to use it constitutionally and consistently," Bratton said. "We are in a position to save lives, reduce injuries, improve safety ... It doesn't get any better than that."

Notes

1. Beck, C., and C. McCue, "Predictive Policing: What Can We Learn From Wal-Mart and Amazon About Fighting Crime in a Recession?" *The Police Chief* 76 (11) (November 2009), http://policechiefmagazine.org/magazine/index.cfm?fuseaction=display_arch&article_id=1942&issue_id=112009.

2. Ibid.

Check out the recap of the Predictive Policing Symposium on the NIJ Web site: http://www.ojp.usdoj.gov/nij/topics/law-enforcement/predictive-policing/symposium/welcome.htm.

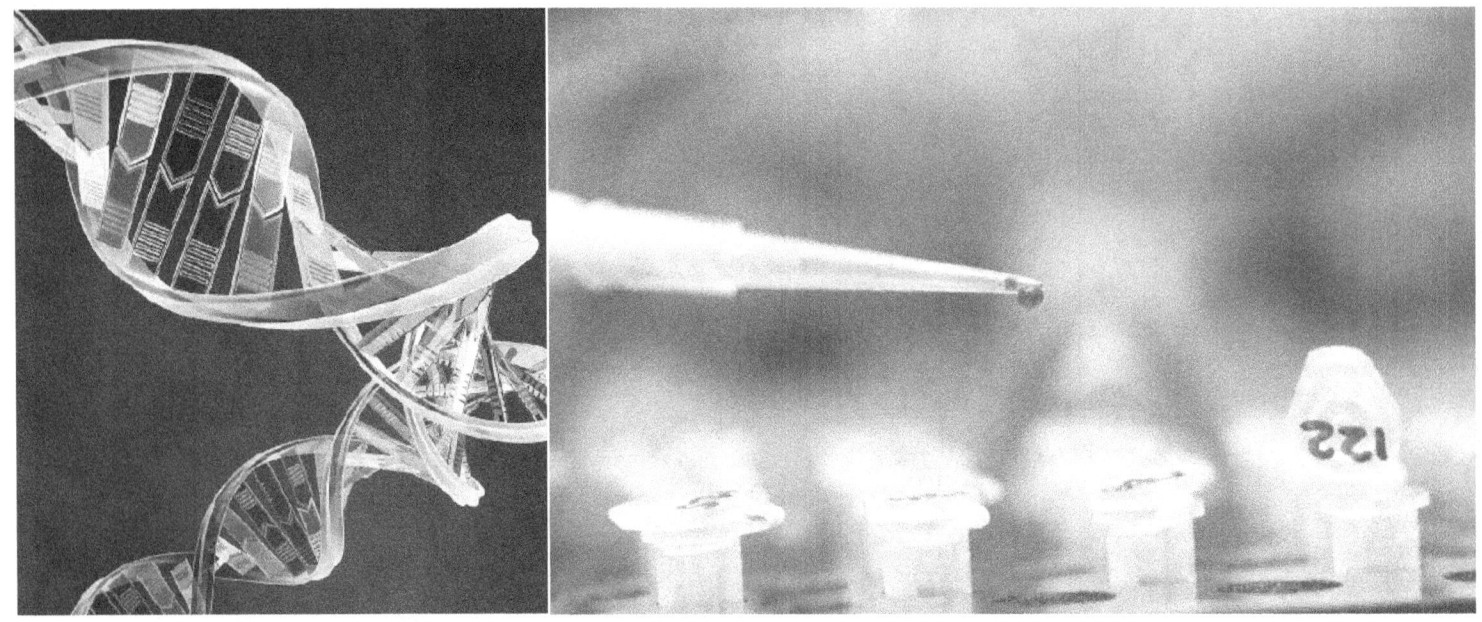

Making Sense of DNA Backlogs — Myths vs. Reality

by Mark Nelson

NIJ addresses the challenge of keeping up with an increasing volume of evidence.

We have all seen the headlines — thousands of untested rape kits have been discovered in law enforcement agencies, and crime laboratories have large backlogs of DNA cases awaiting analysis.

Delays in sending evidence to forensic laboratories and further delays in analysis slow the criminal justice system. In worst-case situations, such delays can contribute to added victimization by serial offenders or imprisonment for people who have not committed a crime.

Why do backlogs persist even after the federal government has spent millions of dollars to address the problem? The backlog picture is complex and requires an understanding of the types of backlogs that exist and the ways crime laboratories work.

What Constitutes a Backlog?

There is no industry wide definition of a backlog. Some laboratories consider a case backlogged if the DNA has not been analyzed after 90 days. Others consider a case backlogged only if the DNA has not been analyzed and the final report sent to the agency that submitted the DNA. The National Institute of Justice defines a backlogged case as one that has not been tested 30 days after it was submitted to the laboratory.

Discussion of and research about backlogs must take into consideration the varying definitions of the

MYTH — Backlogs are a one-time event. As long as one chips away at the backlog of untested cases, it will eventually go away.

term. In addition to delineating length of time, it also is important to identify the type of backlog being referenced. There are two types: (1) casework backlogs and (2) convicted offender and arrestee DNA backlogs.

Casework backlogs. This type of backlog is comprised of forensic evidence collected from crime scenes, victims and suspects in criminal cases and then submitted to a laboratory. Processing this evidence is time-consuming because it must first be screened to determine whether any biological material is present and, if so, what kind of biological material it is. Only then can DNA testing begin. In addition, some samples can be degraded or fragmented or may contain DNA from multiple suspects and victims.

Convicted offender and arrestee DNA backlogs. DNA samples taken from convicted offenders and arrestees pursuant to federal and state laws are significantly easier and faster to analyze than casework samples because they are collected on identical media (usually a paper product). The standardized collection methods in each state allow the laboratory to use automated analysis of many samples at once. Robotic platforms, for example, can process scores of these samples and

the appropriate controls at the same time, generally in a 96-sample format. In addition, unlike with forensic casework samples, the laboratory analyst does not need to "find" the DNA amidst the evidence.

A related but quite different problem involves untested evidence collected from crime scenes and stored in law enforcement evidence rooms that has not been submitted to a crime laboratory for analysis. Recent headlines about backlogs refer to rape kits being stored in law enforcement evidence rooms. NIJ considers untested evidence awaiting submission to laboratories to be a matter separate and different from backlogs in crime laboratories. Federal funding programs to reduce backlogs in crime laboratories are not designed to address untested evidence stored in law enforcement agencies. (See "Untested Evidence: Not Just a Crime Lab Issue" on page 28 of this issue.)

Why Do DNA Backlogs Persist?

Consider the data in figure 1, "DNA Casework: Supply, Demand, Backlogs," and the story they tell about crime laboratory backlogs. Each of the three graphs show DNA backlogs at a particular moment in time. While study methodology differed, each graph portrays the same pattern: even though capacity is increasing, the new cases received by DNA laboratories outpace the ability of laboratories to complete the cases — hence, a backlog.

Today's casework backlog consists of recent cases, not older ones; the backlogged cases from 2004, when Congress passed the DNA Initiative legislation, are gone.[1]

REALITY — Backlogs are not a one-time event. They are dynamic and subject to the law of supply and demand. They may go down, but they may go up.

The bottom line: Crime laboratories have increased their capacity to work cases significantly, but they are not able to eliminate their backlogs because the demand continues to exceed the increases made in capacity.

Why Is Demand for DNA Testing Increasing?

Demand for DNA testing of forensic cases is rapidly increasing for several reasons:

- **Increased Awareness.** Knowledge of the potential of DNA evidence to solve cases has grown exponentially in recent years, not just among professionals in the criminal justice system but also among the general public.

- **Property Crimes.** The number of property crimes being sent for DNA testing is skyrocketing, and property crimes are considerably more common than violent crime. (Most laboratories require violent crime cases to be worked before property crime cases.)

- **Scientific Advances.** Thanks to scientific advances, laboratories can now test smaller DNA samples

Figure 1: DNA Casework: Supply, Demand, Backlogs

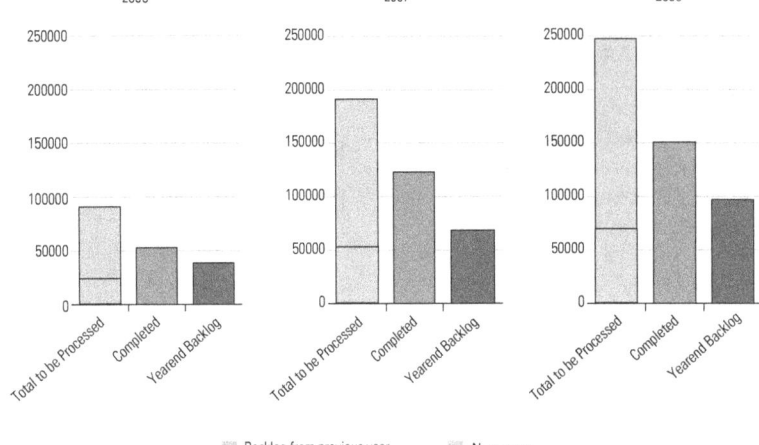

Backlog from previous year   New cases

The federal funding made available through the DNA Initiative has helped state and local governments increase the capacity of their DNA laboratories and decrease backlogs. Without the funds to purchase automated workstations and high-throughput instruments, hire new personnel, and validate procedures that are more efficient, the backlog problem would be much worse. Capacity has yet to reach the increased demand for this testing. Until demand is met, there will continue to be backlogs.

The 2005 graph is based on information from the BJS report "Census of Publicly Funded Forensic Crime Laboratories." In that report, 124 of 187 laboratories that self-identified as handling forensic DNA contributed data. The 2007 graph is based on data reported by 153 of 154 laboratories in the study "2007 DNA Evidence and Offender Analysis Measurement: DNA Backlogs, Capacity and Funding." Data for 2008, reported by applicants for NIJ's 2009 DNA Backlog Reduction Program, came from 109 applicants representing 160 DNA laboratories. (State laboratory systems with multiple DNA laboratories or consortium applications representing more than one laboratory were asked to provide data for all laboratories included in the application.)

Yearend backlog numbers were computed from the information reported by laboratories: the number of cases they had at the beginning of the year plus the number of new requests they received during that year minus the number of those requests that were completed that year.

Sources:

2005–Durose, Matthew R., Census of Publicly Funded Forensic Crime Laboratories, 2005, Washington, DC: US Department of Justice, July 2008, NCJ 222181, www.ojp.usdoj.gov/bjs/content/pub/pdf/cpffc105pdf.

2007–National Forensic Science Technology Center, "2007 DNA Evidence and Offender Analysis Measurement: DNA Backlogs, Capacity and Funding," final report to NIJ from grant 2006-MU-BX-K002, January 2010, NCJ 230328, www.ncjrs.gov/pdffiles1/nij/grants/230328.pdf.

2008–2009 grant applications to DNA Backlog Reduction Program, National Institute of Justice.

■ **Cold Cases.** Many older and unsolved cases from the "pre-DNA" era are being reopened and subjected to DNA testing in hopes of solving them.

■ **Post-Conviction Testing.** Numerous older, pre-DNA cases that resulted in a conviction have been reopened so that DNA testing can be done.

The demand for DNA testing of convicted offenders and arrestee samples, which also is increasing, is being driven by state and federal statutes that require convicted offenders and arrestees to submit DNA samples for testing. As more states pass legislation, there is greater demand for DNA testing of these samples.

What Is Being Done About the Backlog?

In 2004, in response to the emerging backlog, Congress passed the DNA Initiative. The legislation had several objectives, among them to reduce the backlog and build up the nation's database of DNA profiles. By 2010, hundreds of millions of dollars had been spent on efforts toward these goals. Both scientific studies and anecdotal reports confirm that federal funding has made a tremendous impact on the backlog. Without the influx of federal support between 2005 and 2008, the backlog problem would be much worse. Crime laboratories would be completely unable to meet the demand for DNA testing.

Addressing the Casework Backlog

NIJ's largest funding program is the DNA Backlog Reduction Program, which has provided $330 million in direct grants to accredited public-sector DNA laboratories between 2004 and 2009.

than ever before. For example, "touch DNA" samples become available when DNA is transferred by the simple touching of an object. This has led to more requests for DNA testing of guns (to find out who may have handled the weapon) and the swabbing of steering wheels from stolen cars to try to identify the last driver of the car.

What Is CODIS?

The FBI's Combined DNA Index System, known as CODIS, is a software platform that blends forensic science and computer technology.

CODIS has multiple levels where DNA profiles can be stored and searched: the local level (for city and county DNA laboratories), state level and national level.

Data stored at the national level is kept in the National DNA Index System, or NDIS. At this level, an analyst can try to match a DNA profile from a local crime scene sample (also known as a forensic unknown) with an offender's profile from across the nation to solve cases that span states.

Analysts use CODIS to search DNA profiles obtained from crime scene evidence against DNA profiles from other crime scenes and

from convicted offenders and arrestees. CODIS can generate investigative leads in cases when a match is obtained. For example, if the DNA profile from a crime scene matches a sample taken from another crime scene, the cases may be linked in what is called a forensic hit. If the crime scene sample matches a convicted offender or arrestee sample, the result is called an offender hit. Hits give investigating officers valuable information that helps them focus their investigation.

At the end of 2004, CODIS contained just over 2 million offender profiles. As of June 30, 2009, according to FBI reports, more than 7 million offender profiles and 272,000 forensic profiles from crime scene samples had been uploaded to CODIS. The result has been more than 93,000

hits and more than 91,000 investigations aided nationwide.

Learn more about CODIS at the DNA Initiative's Web site: http://www.dna.gov/solving-crimes/cold-cases/howdatabasesaid/codis.

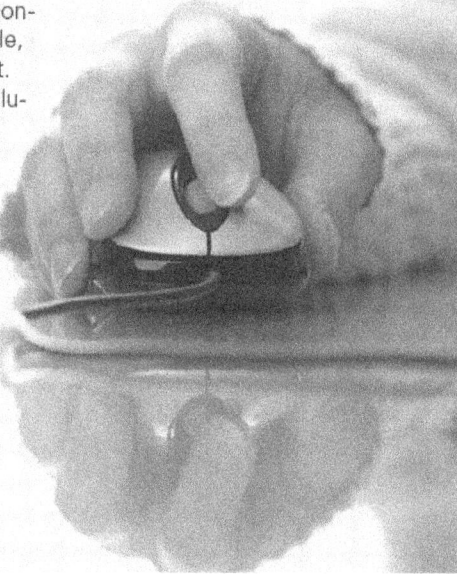

The program's short-term goal is to reduce the backlog of untested cases by providing crime laboratories with funds to work more cases. The crime laboratories can either outsource backlogged cases to private laboratories or test more cases in-house.

The long-term goal is to build the capacity of crime laboratories by providing funds to purchase high-throughput instruments capable of processing multiple samples simultaneously; automated robotic systems; and information management systems to manage the data generated more efficiently and validate newer, more efficient

laboratory procedures. Funds also can be used to hire additional personnel.

According to grant reports submitted to NIJ and surveys of crime laboratories, NIJ's DNA Backlog Reduction Program has helped fund crime laboratories nationwide to reduce backlogs by 135,753 cases. State and local DNA laboratories have significantly increased their capacity to work cases since 2005. Without the federal funds to purchase better equipment and hire additional personnel, many laboratories would not have been able to increase their capacity much beyond the reported 2005 levels.

Without the federal funds to purchase better equipment and hire additional personnel, many laboratories would not have been able to increase their capacity much beyond the reported 2005 levels.

MYTH — If we test every single backlogged case in one huge effort, then we will solve the backlog problem and will never have to deal with it again.

Addressing the Convicted Offender and Arrestee Backlogs

In addition to casework backlogs, there are backlogs in the processing of DNA collected from convicted offenders and arrested persons and the subsequent uploading of the DNA profiles into the national DNA database, called the Combined DNA Index System, or CODIS.

The processes and procedures used in casework DNA testing are very different from those for convicted offenders and arrestees. Thus, the two types of backlogs should be considered and discussed separately to avoid the common mistake of "comparing apples with oranges."

The federal government and all 50 states have laws requiring the collection of DNA samples from individuals convicted of certain crimes. In addition, the federal government and some states have laws concerning the collection of DNA from individuals arrested for certain crimes. DNA profiles from convicted offenders and arrestees are uploaded into CODIS so that law enforcement can compare the DNA gathered from crime scenes against DNA profiles in CODIS. If a match is found, investigators get a lead as to the potential perpetrator of an unsolved crime. Delays in uploading profiles into CODIS could present an opportunity for an offender whose profile is in the system to commit other crimes.

NIJ's program to reduce the backlog of DNA from convicted offenders and arrestees allows laboratories to use grant funds to either process samples in their own facilities or outsource the work to private laboratories. Between 2005 and 2009, NIJ made more than $53.8 million available to reduce the backlog of samples of convicted offenders and arrestees. Federal funding has helped analysts test more than 1.6 million convicted offender and arrestee samples since 2005 and conduct more

REALITY — DNA backlogs will exist until the supply (the capacity of the nation's crime laboratories to test cases) surpasses demand (new service requests).

than 56,000 reviews of the data produced by these analyses. The result has been more than 15,000 CODIS hits.

Figure 2, "Convicted Offender and Arrestee DNA Backlog Data, 2007 and 2008," shows how the

---

Figure 2: Convicted Offender and Arrestee DNA Backlog Data, 2007 and 2008

	2007 Convicted Offender*	2008 Convicted Offender**	2008 Arrestee	2008 Totals (Convicted Offender and Arrestee)
Beginning backlog on January 1	841,847	426,620	28,544	455,164
New samples received	1,021,930	1,267,504	80,609	1,348,113
Samples completed	1,206,612	952,039	57,386	1,009,425

* 2007 data from National Forensic Science Technology Center, *2007 DNA Evidence and Offender Analysis Measurement: DNA Backlogs, Capacity and Funding,* Final report for the National Institute of Justice, Washington, DC: National Institute of Justice, January 2010, NCJ 230328, http://www.ncjrs.gov/pdffiles1/nij/grants/230328.pdf.

** 2008 data provided to NIJ by applicants to the FY 2009 DNA Backlog Reduction Program.

number of convicted offender and arrestee DNA samples sent to and processed by crime laboratories increased dramatically between 2007 and 2008. At the beginning of 2008, the backlog of samples was 455,164. By the end of the year, laboratories had completed analysis of 1 million samples but had received 1.3 million samples — hence, a backlog.

Laboratory capacity to process convicted offender and arrestee DNA, like laboratory capacity to process casework DNA, has increased significantly but not enough to keep pace with the increased demand for this testing. Until demand is met, backlogs will persist.

Mark Nelson is a senior program manager with the Office of Investigative and Forensic Sciences at NIJ.

NCJ 230415

For more information on crime laboratory reports and data:

- Dunrose, M.R., *Census of Publicly Funded Forensic Crime Laboratories, 2005*, Bulletin, Washington, DC: U.S. Department of Justice, Bureau of Justice Statistics, July 2008, NCJ 222181, http://bjs.ojp.usdoj.gov/content/pub/pdf/cpffcl05.pdf.

- National Forensic Science Technology Center, *2007 DNA Evidence and Offender Analysis Measurement: DNA Backlogs, Capacity and Funding*, Final report for the National Institute of Justice, Washington, DC: National Institute of Justice, January 2010, NCJ 230328, http://www.ncjrs.gov/pdffiles1/nij/grants/230328.pdf.

- Cantillon, D., K. Kopiec, and H. Clawson, *Evaluation of the Impact of the Forensic Casework DNA Backlog Reduction Program*, Final report for the National Institute of Justice, Washington, DC: National Institute of Justice, February 2009, NCJ 225803, http://www.ncjrs.gov/pdffiles1/nij/grants/225803.pdf.

Note

1. Some law enforcement agencies are storing untested evidence, such as rape kits, but such untested evidence is not part of the crime laboratory backlog.

Visit NIJ's Web topic page on backlogs at http://www.ojp.usdoj.gov/nij/topics/forensics/lab-operations/evidence-backlogs/welcome.htm.

For information on training, go to http://www.dna.gov/training/#catalog.

DNA backlogs were a topic of discussion at the 2009 NIJ Conference. To listen to the panel, go to http://www.ojp.usdoj.gov/nij/multimedia/audio-nijconf2009-dna-backlog.htm.

Hawaii HOPE

by Philip Bulman

Two evaluations of Hawaii's innovative HOPE program found that participating probationers were significantly less likely to fail drug tests or miss probation appointments. They were also sentenced to less time in prison because of probation revocations than were probationers who did not participate in the program.[1]

Hawaii's Opportunity Probation with Enforcement program uses a "swift and sure punishment" approach to discourage probation violations. Judges give probationers "warning hearings" to tell them that probation terms will be strictly enforced. Frequent, unannounced drug testing is part of the program. Participants must call a hotline each weekday morning to learn if they will be drug-tested that day. Participants who fail a morning drug test are arrested immediately. They may be in court within a few hours, where the judge will change the terms of their probation to include a short stay in jail. Employed probationers are often permitted to serve their jail time on weekends, at least initially, to encourage continued employment.

The court also assures those who need drug treatment or mental health counseling that they will get the treatment they need and are expected to attend and complete such programs. In the past, probationers might skip appointments with probation officers, fail numerous drug tests, or even drop out of treatment programs. Before HOPE, the consequences of

these violations, such as probation revocation and a lengthy prison sentence, were typically delayed and uncertain. The HOPE approach is to respond immediately to probation violations, emphasizing swiftness and certainty rather than severity.

Researchers compared probationers who participated in the HOPE

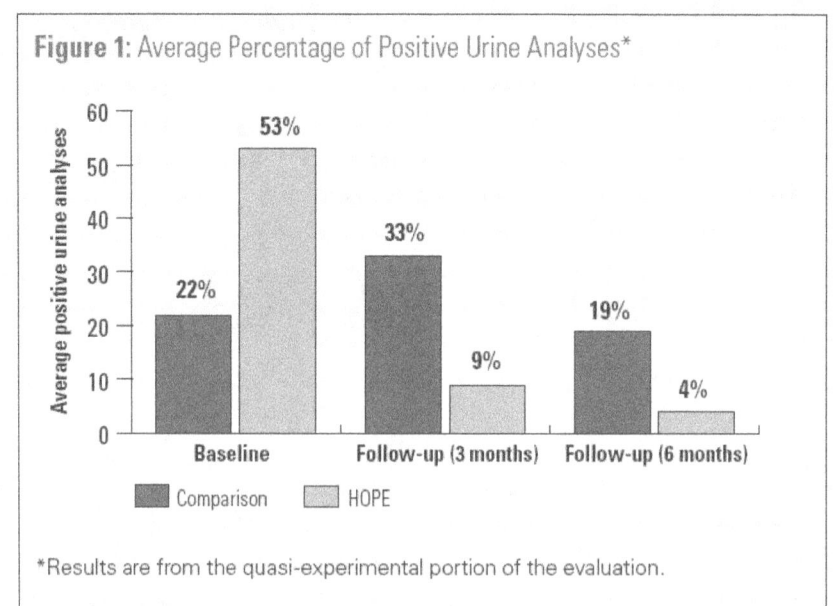

Figure 1: Average Percentage of Positive Urine Analyses*

*Results are from the quasi-experimental portion of the evaluation.

program with those who did not. Results from the NIJ-funded quasi-experimental evaluation show that HOPE probationers had large decreases in positive drug tests and missed appointments. They were much less likely to be arrested. They spent about the same number of

> **The HOPE approach is to respond immediately to probation violations, emphasizing swiftness and certainty rather than severity.**

days in jail for probation violations as the comparison group, serving more frequent but shorter terms. However, they were sentenced to about one-third as many days in prison as the non-HOPE group for probation revocations or new convictions. A one-year randomized controlled trial confirmed these results.

Figure 2: Probationer Outcomes During the One-Year Follow-up Period*

	HOPE	Control
No-shows for probation appointments	9%	23%
Positive urine tests	13%	46%
New arrest rate	21%	47%
Probation revocation rate	7%	15%
Incarceration (days sentenced)	138 days	267 days

*Results are from the one-year randomized controlled trial portion of the evaluation.

During the first three months after HOPE probationers started participating, they showed striking improvement in their drug usage as positive drug tests fell from 53 percent to 9 percent, as figure 1 shows. By contrast, positive drug tests for the non-HOPE group increased initially but showed negligible change over time. Results in figure 2 from the smaller but more rigorous randomized controlled trial show similar declines in problem outcomes among probationers in the HOPE treatment group.

HOPE was pioneered in 2004 by Circuit Judge Steven S. Alm, who believed that the probation system was not working well and could be improved. Initial participants included those whom probation officers thought were particularly high-risk probationers.

Philip Bulman is the editor of the *NIJ Journal.*

NCJ 230416

Note

1. Angela Hawken of Pepperdine University and Mark Kleiman of the University of California, Los Angeles conducted two evaluation studies. One was a quasi-experimental design; the other was a one-year randomized control trial.

Visit NIJ's Web topic page on Hawaii HOPE at: http:// www.ojp.usdoj. gov/nij/topics/ corrections/community/hawaii-hope.htm.

The NIJ final report from the evaluation, Managing Drug Involved Probationers With Swift and Certain Sanctions: Evaluating Hawaii's HOPE *by Angela Hawken and Mark Kleiman, is available at http:// www.ncjrs.gov/pdffiles1/nij/grants/229023.pdf.*

See an interview with Judge Alm at http://www.ojp.usdoj.gov/nij/ journals/media.htm.

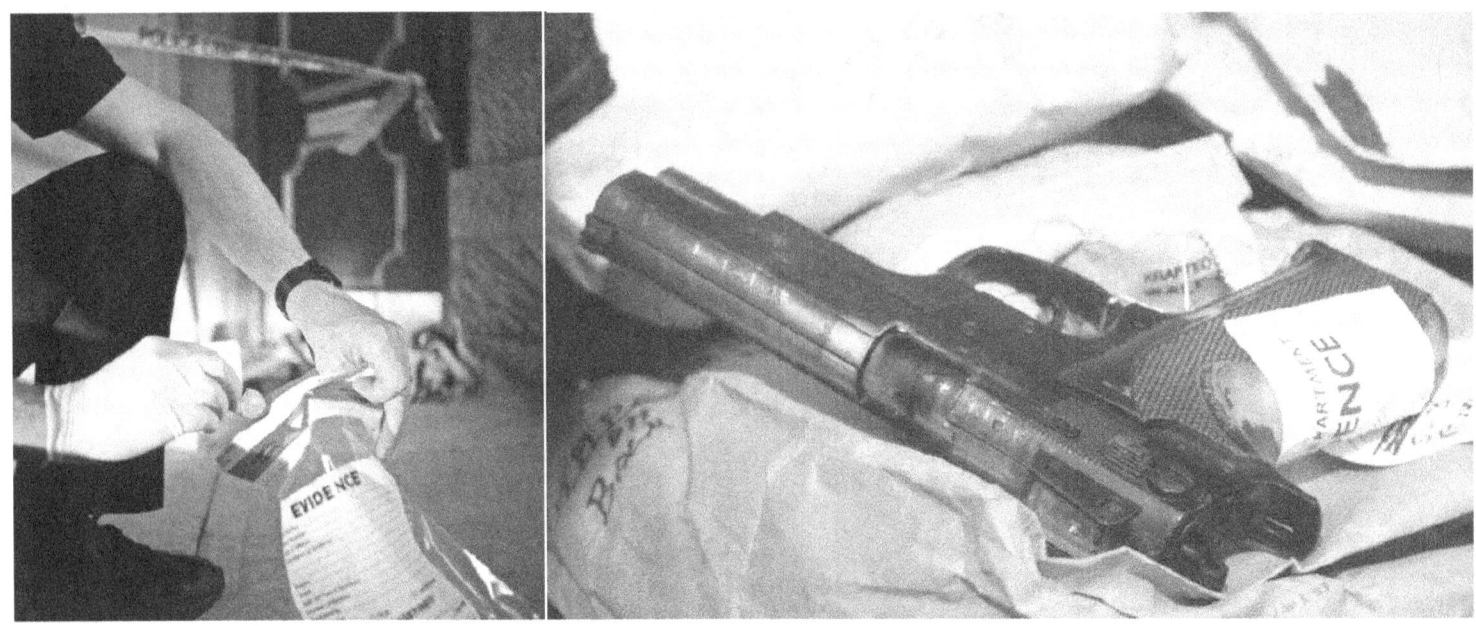

Untested Evidence: Not Just a Crime Lab Issue

by Nancy Ritter

A new study examines forensic evidence caseloads in law enforcement agencies.

The large backlog of evidence awaiting analysis in the nation's crime labs has received much attention of late.

A recent survey funded by the National Institute of Justice and conducted by RTI International looked at a related issue: forensic evidence stored in police property rooms that has not gone to a lab for analysis. Based on a survey of more than 2,000 police departments, researchers determined that forensic evidence existed but had not been sent to a lab in:

- 14 percent of open homicide cases
- 18 percent of open rape cases
- 23 percent of open property crime cases

There are many legitimate reasons why evidence collected from a crime scene would not go to a lab. Evidence may not go to a lab if prosecutors drop the charges against the alleged perpetrator or if someone pleads guilty to the crime. In rape cases, officials may not analyze sperm or other evidence if consent, but not identity, is the contested issue. Finally, some evidence is not sent to the lab because it would not help identify a perpetrator or solve the crime. But these reasons may not explain the entire inventory of unanalyzed property room evidence.

Untested evidence in law enforcement agencies is not considered part of the backlog because it is not actually awaiting analysis in labs. Understanding the policies behind these numbers may help improve how law enforcement uses forensic evidence.

Is There a Knowledge Gap?

Researchers from RTI International asked police departments about forensic evidence that did not go to their crime labs. The survey, which reflects the national situation in 2007, covered fingerprints, firearms, tool marks and biological evidence, including DNA.

The findings suggest that some law enforcement agencies may not fully understand the potential value of forensic evidence in developing new leads in a criminal investigation. For example, police departments cited several reasons for not sending forensic evidence to the lab.

Suspect has not been identified	44%
Suspect was adjudicated without forensic evidence testing	24%
Case was dismissed	19%
Officers did not feel evidence was useful to the case	17%
Analysis was not requested by prosecutor	15%
Suspect was identified but not formally charged	12%
Laboratory was not able to produce timely results	11%
Not enough funds for analysis of forensic evidence	9%
Laboratory would not accept forensic evidence because of backlog	6%

(The above table lists the cited reasons: they could check all that applied.)

The most common reason police do not send evidence to the lab — no suspect identified — may reflect a mindset in some departments that forensic evidence helps in prosecuting a named suspect, but not necessarily in developing new investigatory leads.

This finding is troubling because evidence that contains DNA might identify a suspect through the Combined DNA Index System (CODIS, the national DNA database) even when police have no other clues. Similarly, evidence that contains latent fingerprints might identify an unknown suspect through automated systems like the national Integrated Automated Fingerprint Identification System, or IAFIS. Targeted training could help law enforcement agencies that are not taking advantage of such systems.

Another finding from the survey suggests that some police departments are having trouble prioritizing which evidence to process. For example, 15 percent of the agencies said they did not send evidence to the lab unless a prosecutor requested it. Some jurisdictions may be trying to avoid a seemingly unnecessary use of lab resources by asking the prosecutor to indicate that a case will go forward.

Agencies make such cost-benefit analyses every day as they triage cases. However, some prioritization policies may unwittingly limit opportunities for "no suspect" CODIS hits. Two other key findings related to prioritization, capacity and backlogs are:

- 11 percent of police departments said they did not send evidence to the lab because they felt backlogs prevented timely analysis.

- 6 percent said their lab simply was not accepting new evidence because of a backlog.

> Findings suggest that some law enforcement agencies may not fully understand the potential value of forensic evidence in developing new leads in a criminal investigation.

Evidence Tracking and Retention

One survey goal was to learn how many law enforcement agencies have a computerized information system that can track forensic evidence.

Only 44 percent of law enforcement agencies in the country have such a system. Three out of four large departments (with more than 100 officers) have a computerized tracking system.

With respect to evidence retention policies, the survey found significant variation across jurisdictions. Only 46 percent of the law enforcement agencies said they had a policy requiring the preservation of biological evidence in cases in which the defendant was found guilty. Another 38 percent said they had no such policy, and nearly 16 percent said they were unsure if they had such a policy.

Where to From Here?

How many of the unsolved cases with forensic evidence might be solved — or yield investigative leads — if a lab analyzed evidence currently in police custody?

The survey did not try to answer this question, but it merits more investigation. Indeed, the researchers recommended more study, including a scientific, "best-practices" look at how, considering current financial realities, such cases should be prioritized for testing. This would include how to solve the greatest number of cases, help the greatest number of victims to reach closure, and bring the worst criminals to justice.

The survey also did not address unsolved cases in which evidence was previously analyzed to no avail but which now — with the benefit of larger offender databases and new forensic technologies — might yield leads or be solved. For example, a latent print run through IAFIS several years ago with no successful match might result in a match if resubmitted today.

Any overall increase in forensic evidence sent to crime labs for analysis will have an impact on existing backlogs. With property crimes, for instance, collecting and analyzing DNA evidence can have a significant effect on arrests and prosecutions. An NIJ-funded five-city field test in 2008 showed that collecting and analyzing DNA evidence in burglaries resulted in new investigatory leads, more arrests and higher closure rates.[1] However, the burden of collecting, analyzing and acting on DNA evidence from every burglary would be cataclysmic for some police departments, crime labs, prosecutors and legal aid defense lawyers

without a major infusion of additional resources. Moreover, burglaries are just a start. All told, there were more than 4.5 million unsolved property crimes in 2007. Any one of these crimes could potentially yield forensic evidence. Jurisdictions need to consider the costs and benefits of policies that involve DNA testing for all property crimes.

Based on data from the survey, the researchers made the following recommendations:

- Standardize evidence retention policies.

- Train police in the benefits and use of forensic evidence, including guidelines or protocols on prioritizing cases for lab analysis.

- Create — or improve — computerized systems to track forensic evidence.

- Improve storage capacity for analyzed and unanalyzed forensic evidence.

- Develop a system wide approach to improve coordination among the police, forensic lab and prosecutor's office. This could include dedicated staff for case management, regular team meetings for case review, and computerized systems to allow information-sharing across agencies.

Besides thinking about how some of these recommendations might work, it may be important to pay greater attention to small- to mid-sized

> An NIJ-funded five-city field test in 2008 showed that collecting and analyzing DNA evidence in burglaries resulted in new investigatory leads, more arrests and higher closure rates.

police departments. The survey revealed, for example, that police agencies with fewer than 50 officers accounted for nearly three out of 10 unsolved rape cases that contain unanalyzed forensic evidence. As the researchers note, larger agencies may have more capacity (staff to apply for and manage evidence processing and testing grants) than smaller agencies, but small agencies have a significant contribution to make in solving crimes and successfully prosecuting criminals.

Read the full report of *The 2007 Survey of Law Enforcement Forensic Evidence Processing*, which offers new insight into this issue: http://www.ncjrs.gov/pdffiles1/nij/grants/228415.pdf.

Nancy Ritter is a writer with the National Institute of Justice.

NCJ 230417

Note

1. Ritter, N., "DNA Solves Property Crimes (But Are We Ready for That?)" *NIJ Journal* (261) (October 2008), http://www.ojp.usdoj.gov/nij/journals/261/dna-solves-property-crimes.htm; Roman, J.K., S. Reid, J. Reid, A. Chalfin, W. Adams, and C. Knight, *The DNA Field Experiment: Cost-Effectiveness Analysis of the Use of DNA in the Investigation of High-Volume Crimes,* Final report for the National Institute of Justice, Washington, DC: National Institute of Justice, April 2008, NCJ 222318, http://www.ncjrs.gov/pdffiles1/nij/grants/222318.pdf.

Visit NIJ's Web topic page on backlogs at http://www.ojp.usdoj.gov/nij/topics/forensicslab-operations/evidencebacklogs

The Stockholm Prize in Criminology

David Weisburd Wins the Stockholm Prize in Criminology

The National Institute of Justice congratulates Dr. David Weisburd, winner of the 2010 Stockholm Prize, for his groundbreaking work in hot spots policing.

The Stockholm Prize in Criminology is an international prize sponsored by the Swedish Ministry of Justice. It is awarded for "outstanding achievements in criminological research or for the application of research results by practitioners for the reduction of crime and the advancement of human rights."[1]

Weisburd's work in hot spots policing emphasizes the role of place — not people — as the key unit of analysis for crime prediction and prevention. His NIJ-funded research, largely focused on crime in specific places like Jersey City, N.J., and Seattle, shows that crime can drop substantially in small hot spots without rising in other areas.

Weisburd has produced evidence to show that the introduction of a crime-prevention strategy in a small, high-crime area often creates a "diffusion of benefits" to nearby areas, reducing crime (rather than increasing it) in the immediate zone around the target area. His work further suggests that crime patterns depend not just on criminals but also on policing in key places and other factors such as the placement of fences, alleys and other environmental features.

Jim Bueermann, chief of police at the Redlands Police Department in California, said Weisburd has been enormously influential. "David's work has contributed substantially to the body of theoretical work about crime control. He has also helped police departments understand and utilize more evidence-based approaches to controlling crime. As a 31-year veteran of policing, I know the value of practitioner-oriented, crime-control research and how it can dramatically advance the effectiveness of policing strategies. David's work has forever altered the way I view policing. His inspirational efforts have directly led to the addition of a police criminologist in my department and a reframing of our policing model to reflect a science-based approach," he said.

To learn more about Dr. Weisburd's research read the NIJ report, *Mapping Crime: Understanding Hot Spots:* http://www.ncjrs.gov/pdffiles1/nij/209393.pdf.

—Yolanda Curtis, special assistant to the Director of the National Institute of Justice.

NCJ 230418

Note

1. The Stockholm Criminology Symposium, "About the Stockholm Prize," http://www.criminologyprize.com/extra/pod/?id=12&module_instance=3&action=pod_show&navid=12. March 22, 2010.

Visit NIJ's Web topic page on hot spots policing at http://www.ojp.usdoj.gov/nij/topics/law-enforcement/hot-spot-policing/welcome.htm.

See a video of Dr. Weisburd and Deputy Assistant Attorney General Mary Lou Leary discuss hot spots: http://www.ojp.usdoj.gov/nij/journals/media.htm.

Search. Match. Solve.

NamUs: National Missing and Unidentified Persons System

NamUs is the nation's first online repository for missing persons and unidentified decedents records. The system is two databases:

Missing Persons Database

- Anyone — law enforcement and the loved ones of a missing person — can add a case; cases go through a verification process before they are posted.
- Anyone can search the database.
- Resources include geo-mapping technology to locate police and medical examiner offices and links to state clearinghouses, Attorneys General offices and state laws.

www.findthemissing.org

Unidentified Decedents Database

- Anyone can search the database using factors such as unique physical characteristics (tattoos, scars, implants), dental information, clothing and forensics data.
- Only medical examiners and coroners can enter cases.

www.identifyus.org

www.NamUs.gov

NamUs is funded by the National Institute of Justice in a partnership with the National Forensic Science Technology Center.

What You Can Do

- Raise awareness within your agency or your community about NamUs and its resources.
- Encourage your state missing persons clearinghouse to use NamUs to help solve cases.
- Encourage medical examiners and coroners to enter their cases at www.identifyus.org.

The databases have been linked for simultaneous searching and matching of cases.

Watch a six-minute video:

NamUs Behind the Scenes: How It Works, Why It Matters

www.findthemissing.org/homes/ how_it_works_video

National Missing and Unidentified Persons System
NamUs

missing 3-11-07

missing 10-7-0

missing 3-8-07

missing 5-9-0

The National Institute of Justice is the research, development and evaluation agency of the U.S. Department of Justice. NIJ's mission is to advance scientific research, development and evaluation to enhance the administration of justice and public safety.

The National Institute of Justice is a component of the Office of Justice Programs, which also includes the Bureau of Justice Assistance; the Bureau of Justice Statistics; the Community Capacity Development Office; the Office for Victims of Crime; the Office of Juvenile Justice and Delinquency Prevention; and the Office of Sex Offender Sentencing, Monitoring, Apprehending, Registering, and Tracking (SMART).